THE G.A.P

Thank You
4 The
Support

Paul "Phroze"

poetry4youdig.com

Written by: Paul "Phroze" Munson

Not Just Alphabets Publishing

Fort Worth, Texas

All Not Just Alphabets Publishing titles, Phrozen Productions, imprints and lines distributed are available at special quantity discounts for bulk purchases for sales promotion, fund raising, premiums, educational, institutional and library use.

Printed in the U. S. A.

Library of Congress Catalog Card Number: 0996312990

ISBN: 978-0-9963129-9-8

Cover Design by: Devie Perry

The Gospel According to Paul

Dedication

I dedicate this book to my beautiful wife and two daughters for all their love, patience and support. I dedicate this book to my mother for inspiring me to become the writer that I am still becoming every day and I dedicate this book to both of my parents for showing me not to be afraid to speak in front of an audience. I dedicate this book to my two brothers and sister for all of their love and support. I dedicate this book to Brant Hudson and Jay "Roller" Bennett for believing in me and always requesting to hear what I had written even in my rough draft phases. (Rest in peace) I dedicate this book to the rest of my family and friends for all of their support along the way. Last but not least, I dedicate this to all of my past and present teachers and experiences for giving me the gospel that I have to share.

Introduction

One definition of gospel is infallible truth or as a guiding principle.

With that being said; in this book, I plan to give insight into part of the

journey that I have traveled. I am sure you can relate to many of the

moments I have lived, thought about, and eye witnessed.

Contents

Chapter 1

In The Beginning

In the beginning, there was more that you and I will ever know; however, we have learned a lot along the way. For the rest of our lives, we will be learning. One should never think that they know it all. When this is the case, you can no longer grow. I have learned that you must believe in yourself even when no one else does. You must encourage yourself even when no one else does. Some of the very people that you think wish you well, can't wait for you to have a down fall. Be aware of the company you keep. Stop giving energy to people's negative opinions about you. Continue to progress toward the reality that you truly desire. Stop blaming everyone else for your problems. When you point your finger at someone else, you have three fingers pointing back at you. Start working on the solutions.

How are you doing? I am not the one to be assuming, so I thought I would ask. Did you answer this question slow or fast? Are you for certain about how you feel? When is the last time you had a decent meal? When is the last time someone said that they loved you because I do not have a clue? When is the last time that you were able to get a new pair of shoes? When is the last time you cried just from looking at the news? Are you feeling sad, mad, frustrated, irritated or is everything going ok? Do you have a place to stay? Are most of your loved ones still living? Do you do more taking than giving? Has your heart been broken by the one you love? Do you think of pretty things like a flower or a dove? Do you travel by bus, by car, or do you walk near and far? Do you find yourself always alone? Does anyone ever call your cell phone just to talk or only to collect on a bill? Please, just tell me how you feel. Do people come by just to visit or do you hate to even say, "Who is it" because folks always want to borrow your money? Do people even recognize that you are lonely? I am just wondering because I see stress on your face. I will not know until I hear your case.

Does anyone listen when you talk or turn their head and start to walk? Is your body healthy and are your pockets wealthy? Of course; if you had dividends, you would have a lot of friends until the money ran out. This is when they no longer know about you but the next rich man. When people hold your hand, do they feel nervous and tense? I know some people don't have any sense. How many months are you behind in rent? Is all of your money spent on the children, lights, telephone, water, and gas? Are you accepted or labeled an outcast? When times are hard, do they get worse? Are you hungry? Do you thirst? If life was a quiz, what would be your grade? Are you doing bad or do you have it made? When will you let go of your negative past and how long will you last? If you asked me how I was doing, you would not really want to know. It is like a balloon with a hole in it that I still try to blow. It seems as if I get closer to the ground but I still try to smile and not frown. You should try to smile sometimes because it will relax your mind.

In other words, you must stay positive as can be. It is true that negative thoughts will come to you but you must teach yourself to eliminate those thoughts. I know it is hard but you have to try. You usually get whatever you think. If you think negative, don't expect positive results. It is totally up to you. At the end of the day, you can only thank yourself for your out- comes. God gives us intellect to make the right choices in life but for some reason, we still don't listen at times and that gets us in trouble. I know it is rough out there and no matter how positive you are some things still end up in a negative situation. Could it be that God wants you to appreciate the "ups" when they do come by taking you through the "downs"?

The journey in life has valleys and mountains. You have to go through the valleys to get to the mountain tops. Life is all about ups and downs. Some people stay in valleys though because they start to feel sorry for themselves; which in turn, starts to make them always choose sorry choices. At the same time; they say things like, I am just holding on and waiting on my blessing to fall from Heaven. You can't just sit around waiting for a hand out or a drop out. You have to work out. God needs to see you putting forth some effort. I heard "Nick Cannon" say in an interview, "you have to be a self-motivator because people will always come against you. You also have to be a self-generator. You have to create your own opportunity". Your blessing will come but you must first, get up and get busy.

Come inside and look at it through my eyes. Watch out for drunk drivers because you might get hit. Live life to the fullest before "death" comes to kiss. Don't close your eyes because when they open, there could be an unpleasant surprise. You might witness someone being shot. You might not want to finish everything you start. That lady over there is crying because her mom, brother, and cousin are all dying. Don't text and drive because you might wreck. If you haven't started gambling, I advise you to not start the bets. That small excuse of a man hit her in the eye, right after he promised her she would die. Keep your eyes open and watch for all things. Thieves are greedy. They want the wallet, watch, car, and the ring. There go four young brothers in a car. I wonder how far they will go before they are pulled over by a "dirty cop". Oops, I spoke a little too soon. They just got stopped.

That 13 year old girl just had her first baby and the 18 year old daddy is acting "shady". She may have a disease that can't be cured. She is scared; will not go to the doctor, so she stays unsure. That little child just called his mother a "bastard." Times are changing faster and faster. One of my high school team mates committed suicide. I wonder if people had paid more attention, would he still be alive. I'm just telling you what my eyes have seen out there. You have to keep fighting even if you don't think life is fair. At the same time, they just cut off my water, gas, and electricity. Why do they give criminals so much publicity? The media is purposely negative. Many times you have to actually be there to see news that is positive. Some politicians

14

are the biggest criminal dealers. Some policeman are "trigger happy human killers." He didn't get that job because his hair was too long. Her boyfriend broke up with her with a text through the cell phone. They would not let him in the club because they stereotyped him, calling him a thug. The gangs have been brain washed to kill each other. The original gangs protected their communities of sisters and brothers. A lot of my peers are in jail. A lot of them got life in that "hell". Some of my classmates died young and quick. They died for many reasons, not just from a gun that clicks. It can be rough looking through these eyes but hopefully it makes me more wise. Through all of this, I still have to stay as positive as can be. I understand that it is totally up to me.

I've seen a whole lot in these young years that I have lived. I do not take life for granted any more. I lost an uncle to a drunk driver when I was 8 years old. He had come home to visit us in "Fort Worth" and was headed back to school. It was my uncle's senior year at "Jarvis Christian College". Someone was having trouble with their car on the side of the road and my uncle, Michael stopped to help. He seemed to always help people. As he was doing what he normally does, a drunk driver ended his Earthly walk, this time around. It was one of the hardest things for me to deal with at that age. I learned early, to give it all I have before it ends. Before I graduated high school, I lost about 18 school mates. It got to a point to where I just wondered, "who would die this month". I started to value my life at an early age. I love getting older because it means, I am not dead. I have friends and family that will not get out of jail for a long time and some will not get out at all. I've seen people lose their mind because of drugs. I've witnessed gang violence. I have been evicted and I have been robbed. That is not all I've seen but I am just giving you a few examples of why I don't take life for granted anymore.

How long will it be for us to have unity and stop the killing? When will we show love with our feelings? How long will it be before I can drive a car or become a star? How long will his girlfriend treat him bad? How long will my mother stay sad? Will people ever stop stabbing in the back? The system has people hooked on crack. Too many people are jealous of the next man. It only takes common sense to understand. I am an entrepreneur but if "push comes to shove", I will work a minimum wage job. At gun point; my family, was robbed. We kept on going even though we struggled to survive. I thank God that I am even still alive.

A husband is weak when he does not have respect for his wife. I wish young people cared more about their life. Some men are quiet but are getting beat up by their lady and there are too many babies having a baby. Wars will never cease. Some will never have peace. Some sorry baby makers refuse to help take care of the child. Instead, they stay in the streets and act wild. How long will it be? Ask yourself this question and try to learn a lesson. I am just trying to bring the truth. You must eventually grow out of your youth. How long will that be?

It is totally up to you. You do not want to go to the grave with your life's purpose not done. You have to become the person that you are supposed to be. You never know who you are an example to. There are people watching you and learning from you that you will never know. Life is too short to not take it serious. Stop being attracted to so much foolishness. This slows you down. Live your dream and let other people get their own dreams. The only person you have to prove something to is, yourself. Everybody goes through tribulations. I know things are on your mind. I feel what you are going through 100% but still, keep pushing!

You all just don't understand. I have some major stuff on my mind. I am serious. I am not lying. I am more serious than a heart attack. Sometimes, you have to separate from the pack. I try not to abuse the alcohol. I need to do away with it all. They just buried my 23rd friend. He never saw the age 2 times 10. I just pawned my d v d player and microwave, all because my rent was too late. I'm broke but being pressured to buy the house. I'm trying to stay humble and quiet like a mouse but I want to scream so bad! I don't keep in touch like I should with my dad. As far as that goes, I don't keep in enough touch with many. My money seems so close to empty. Some of my so called "potnas" really love to hate. I keep coming real every time they come fake. Some of my female friends hate also. They do it. They smile in my face and think I don't know. My little cousin is left with a very major decision. They want her to pull the plug on her mother that is barely living. Many of my people are so stressed out. Many times, I want to go right but end up taking the wrong route. Every bill I have is behind. Around me, there seems to be so much crime. I have too many love ones in jail. Many times when I strive to succeed, I often fail. My job treats me like a "modern day slave". I am not trying hard enough to get paid but I know that is my own fault. Against me, this ignorant banger tried to assault. I have warrants that used to be tickets. I wrecked my car. I hope I can deal with it. Everybody and "they mama" seems to need my help but I'm in the same boat. I can't do this by myself. I'm stressed. He's stressed. She's stressed. We are all stressed but all we have to do is pass the test. For some reason, I let things bother me like frustration, aggravation, messed up situations, irritation, lack of motivation, complications, tribulations, and not having a wii or a play station. All and all, I'm cool though because I have been through worse before. This stuff on my mind needs to leave so I will not think about it anymore.

It can be rough but you must keep going. The only person that can ever stop you, is you. Do not do that to yourself. You deserve better. Stay strong no matter how bad your situation is at the moment. You must stay focused on making life better for yourself. When you make life better for yourself, you make life better for those around you. Never become satisfied. Don't get greedy, but never become finished. Always want to improve yourself more. This is a life long journey that we are on. Walk carefully and pay attention to your surroundings at all times.

Chapter 2

No Time To Waste

Some people are on different levels. Some are "Godly" and some are "devils". Some are smart and some are dumb. Some are too serious and some have too much fun. Some are high and some are sober. Some are sisters and some are brothers. Many are lovers. Others are haters. Some are real parents and others are just baby makers. It is hard to understand some of these folks. Many people take life for a joke. You might not be able to handle being rich if you have always been broke. Some are positive and some have no hope. Everybody will not feel what you have to say. Even though we all need it, some refuse to meditate and pray. No matter what you have been taught, there is always so much more. Even if you are a Christian, your intuition tells you that "Jesus" is not going to ever be physically knocking at your door. Even if he did; you not ready so, you might just let him continue to knock. Just because you tell the truth, does not mean that the masses will flock. Negative people will always go against the positive one. Some proclaimed winners have not really won. Stop wasting breath on deaf ears. Numbered are our years. We have children to look after. Some grown folks wish you disaster. You have to stay strong. What is really right, some think is wrong. Some people are not as advanced as you are. Don't try to pull people near that want to be far. You have too much business to take care of. Everybody that say they love you, does not really have love.

One thing that I have had to learn is to humble myself. We are always growing. I now understand that some people might not catch on to my opinions. It used to really frustrate me that people that were around me, just wouldn't get it. I finally understood that some are not necessarily supposed to get it and I do not have to necessarily get what they believe. We can agree to disagree. We can only be accountable for ourselves. We are all at different points on the life road that we travel. I now understand and that helps me have peace. That is one reason why I try to put myself around people that know more than I do. I am teacher but I am even a better student. We are all enrolled in life school for the rest of our lives.

We don't have time to waste. I only have one day left, so what should I do? I am asking me, not you. I don't know if there will be a tomorrow. This day I live has been borrowed. Two roads have been given to me. Which one will be followed? Lord, thank you for this one day. Will I handle my business or will I play? I have one day to take care of what has to be done. There is only one day left for this God's son. Handling my business can be fun. I just have one day left to mess up or do right. I only have one day left to come out of the darkness into the light. What do I do? Peer pressure for me, is too much pressure for a fact. I need to work and stop just hanging around like bats. I only have one day left. I have to do it and not have too much pride to accept help. Will I keep it real or will I be fake? I must take this day serious because my life is always at stake.

Just imagine if you had only 24 hours to live. If that was all I had, I would reflect on the life I lived. I would settle all disputes with my enemies. I would have no more envy. I would say, "good bye" to family and friends. I would also pray that my life wouldn't end. I would increase my insurance policy so my family could benefit. I would evaluate how my life was spent. I would be scared as a," I don't know what". I would wish that time would freeze and get stuck. I would try to stop all my love ones' cries. I wouldn't go to sleep. There would be no more blinks from my eyes. I would update and edit my will. I would pray to God and see if we could make a deal. I know that time waits on no one. If I had 24 hours to live, I would be too serious to have any fun.

My life might not be complete but it would be done. I would check with science to see if I could be cloned because I wouldn't be ready to go. I would try to go read this poem at an open mic show. I would try to do everything that should have been done in these young years. No one knows when their time will come so I better step up my gears. I better take care of my business; yea, I better. My life could be gone forever and when it's my time, I want to go with no regrets. I'm ready to start writing my own checks. I am going to start living like I only have 24 hours to live. I am not ready to go anywhere and that is just what that is. The Lord knows, I hope I have more than 24 hours to live.

God has given me so many chances. There are many times that I could have taken an exit from the building (died). I've worked hard for a long time. I used to get very little sleep. I had become immune to being somewhat of a "zombie". I would have a conversation with you but never know it. I used to be so sleepy trying to work 3 jobs. I did not have a car so I rode the bus to my day time jobs and walked or rode my bike to my night time job. I can't tell you how many times I fell asleep on the bus, missed my destination and had to get off the bus and walk back. Once your body is worn out, it does not care how much you give it to try and trick it to not be tired. The body will shut down with or without your permission. I am almost embarrassed to write this but I used to walk in the middle of the street on purpose to my night time job for two reasons. I could hear the dogs barking but could not see them. I figured that the middle of the street was safer and I kept a stick, just in case I needed to swing on those dogs. It is rough hearing the bark but not being able to see the dog. The other reason is because, I would close my eyes and count to ten every other ten seconds and that would allow me to get some sleep on my way to work while I was walking. I opened my eyes to make sure I was not running into any curves on the street and to make sure cars were not coming (crazy right). I am now a witness that this is not getting any sleep at all. Just imagine how my life became a wreck when I finally got me a car.

We don't value time like we should. These hours don't belong to us. "The Nameless One" lets us use this time. That is why we must value every moment. Wouldn't you hate for your children to waste their life? I think God sees us like that. Time is ticking folks.

You hear people say things like, "I'm just killing time". You can't kill time. Time may be the one thing that lives forever. People often say, "this sure is a long day". This day is actually the same length as it was the day before. In other words, don't waste your blessed time. You are waiting on the right time but the right time is not waiting on you. The right time is always, now.

We don't have time to waste people. I must not put off what needs to be done today because tomorrow might not ever come. The fight is not over. I have not yet won. Sometimes, it's not what you know but who you know, you see. I need to think twice before I try to get in the industry. I'm not going to jump the gun. I'm waiting for the count of 1, 2, and 3. I don't want to drown so I have to stop "throwing a fit". You all might not know but God knows I want to go legit. I should have had my books out by now. I know this. I know what it takes for the industry to give me a kiss but forget the kiss; I need to take care of some stuff. I know it takes work. I can not bet it all on luck because I have not necessarily been too lucky. My pockets are too flat. I am ready for them to get "bulky". I know that I am supposed to be in the studio. I know I need a good manager, producer, promoter, and lawyer to help "Phroze". I know there are other people I need that I don't even know. I need a mentor to mentor me about my shows. I don't have to go to a building to have church. I need to get this residual income and leave this temporary work. I can call out the temp service because I work there. They got me packing boxes and unloading trucks while the boss sits with a stare. I just get tired of living from check to check. If I don't get it right, I'm going to wreck. I don't want to live hustle to hustle either. I got to get back to the basics and be a "block bleeder". I need to go to sleep or at least take a nap. My body is tired. I have to quit treating it like, I'm mad. I have popped too many "no dose". I am glad that I am no longer hooked on those. I used to drop them in my "monster energy drinks". My eyes would get stuck open. I couldn't even blink and if it is not what you know but who you know, can I get one of you "cats" to come know "Phroze".

I know the door is open but I am still on the outside looking in. I need my present situation to end and my new one to begin. Plus; it's more than me. I have family to look after. I can't start the next one until I turn the page from the first chapter. In the industry, I know there is room for one more. Instead of working for it, I want to own the store. Instead of buying a ticket, I want to own the jet or plane. I wouldn't mind owning the yacht or the train. I am just trying to get in. Can someone give me the key? Dear God, can you help me please? I am just trying to get in the industry.

I also now understand that if I don't get in the industry, it is just fine. At the same time; in a way, I am already in the industry. I guess I am on the ground level or maybe even underground in the basement and that is ok. I know I will always work and pray on my purpose. I know God guides me and protects me. The industry might not be for everybody but if it is for me, I know God will let me in. I will be patient and keep bringing the words of my wisdom. As long as I do what I am supposed to do, I will end up exactly where I am supposed to be. "Can you dig it?"

Chapter 3

The Voice Of The Unheard

The voice of the unheard is who I am. I don't believe my culture is cursed because of someone named, "Ham". You can always find racism on the job. Your intentions were to feed your children when they caught you rob. Most people are criminals. They just have not been caught. Most of you all are scared to talk about what you saw. That little girl was raped but don't know what to say because that is the same thing she sees happen to her "crack head" mama every other day. Some mothers are scared of their own daughters and sons. Some people feel they have to sleep with their gun. They don't know when it will have to be used. That captain was wrong that "bailed out" on that cruise. One thing that always has to happen is change. Some "cats" get more love from their gang. Some churches have the biggest hypocrites. To make it worse, a lot of them are in the pull pit. "2 Pac" already told you that "Brenda had a baby". I know most women drive men crazy and I know we men do the same. Children that disrespect their parents should be ashamed. God makes you pay for your lack of respect. Every 1st and 15th day of the month, she waits on a check. The victims of "Hurricane Katrina" were treated like a foreign country. It is hard out here when you don't have any money. Life can be hard and that is not funny. I was a "player" but I was lonely. I didn't know how to trust folks. His brain is on drugs like the dude in the commercial with the egg yoke. Some politicians and preachers are pimps.

Dudes that beat up on women are wimps. They can't afford the house they stay in. You are a woman but you want to be a man. He sleeps with one eye open. He is in the ghetto wishing and hoping. He gets tired of almost getting shot and we all know, "you can't trust all cops." Half of you all can't trust yourself. You talk about it but do you really want wealth? If you do, why aren't you trying to get it? She really is sorry for the time that she cheated. We don't support our own stores. Some of you all are riding the elevator but won't get off because you are scared to go to a higher floor. You are a monster like "Cookie". You are a veteran at being a rookie. If you look for it, you will find trouble. Women want to but most men don't want to cuddle. That family has nowhere to live. He gave an offering but really didn't want to give. For many, being married is great and for others, it just "ain't". Children in other countries are not the only ones that need food. There are children right here that don't know what they gone do. Listen to those that are silent. They get tired of getting told to be quiet.

There are a lot of people in our own communities that need our help. I am not talking about those that don't try to help themselves. The truth is, it is rough out here. A lot of people are going through the same thing right now. Peoples' lives have really changed in a short period of time. People have been laid off their jobs. People have been fired. Houses have been lost to for closer. 401k plans have disappeared. Cars have been repossessed. People are really struggling. People are hungry so crime increases. We have to make life better. It is up to us to pull together to make this place a better place.

Stop depending on corrupt leaders. Do your part.

To our intuition, we need to learn to listen. It is totally up to you to pay attention. There are a few things I would like to mention. First of all, ignore anyone that is "hating on you and dissing". Don't be selfish. Offer an extension. Your prayers should be more "thanks" instead of "Christmas list wishing". "Tail" is what you should never be kissing. I believe people are judging when they say, "you are not going to Heaven if you are not Christian". If the "slave controllers" pull you over, don't be "tripping". Your personal show has already begun. Sit back. Read a little bit. Have some fun. We are all the Creator's daughters and sons. Forget being number two. Always go for number one. Be well rounded like a circle, not an octagon. For my lady, I am fond. The Lord helps you fight the battle so the war will be won. We were taught to give it to God and it is already done but in reality, we too have to work like the "Only Begotten Sun". On knowledge, get "sprung". Into prosperity, take a plunge. Soak wisdom up like a sponge. Strive to make yourself better. Stay strong through the stormy weather. Listen to your spirit. You don't have to wait till Sunday morning to try and hear it.

Always remember, that there was life here before anyone wrote any book and I do mean any book. My ancestors listened to their spirit. Without, any human teaching you anything, your spirit always talks to you. There is something inside of you that tells you if something is good or bad for you. Many times we still choose bad and then complain about not going with our first mind. Your first mind is that spirit. It is your intuition. The same "first mind" that tells you to get out the street because a car is coming is the same one you ignore at other times. Take other times as serious as you take getting out of that street. As long as you are in your right mind, the "first mind" usually works toward your good.

I got myself in it, so I have to deal with it. I have to take care of my business. No one can hide. "The Almighty" is the witness. I must not point the finger at no one but myself. "Dear Lord", please help? It is time to stop playing games and read the books on the shelf. It is time to stop blaming others for my mistakes. It is time to be real with myself and stop coming fake. It is time to walk across the ocean and stop drowning in this lake. There is more out there than meets the eye. I have to serve my purpose while I live before I die. I have the potential to do more than just get by. "The Creator" has blessed us with so much already. I just got to hold on when the boat rocks and doesn't seem so steady. I must fear no man. I don't care if his name is "Jason or Freddy". A man must not keep himself in debt so I must jump out. I must take care of mine and not worry about somebody else's house. I got to get up and do something and stop just sitting on the couch. I got myself in it so I have to "handle up". My conversation can't be any "ifs, ands, or buts. I have to change my ways and get up. I refuse to get stuck.

I have learned to take responsibility for my actions. Whatever situations I am in, is because this is what I have attracted in one way or another. I believe in karma to the fullest. I believe that, what goes around comes around. I used to try to be "slick" and have had to pay for every bit of it. Stay strong. Pray to the "Creator" but you must put in the work. You must do what has to be done. No one feels sorry for you. Feeling sorry for you doesn't encourage you to work on your situation. You can't just sit around and wait for it to happen. You have to get off of your butt and make it happen.

Chapter 4

I Have Got To Get Better

Without drinking, he felt drunk like everything was moving. He doesn't want to make a butt out of anyone, so he is not assuming. He is almost 33 years old like the number of "Patrick Ewing". He tries everyday but he really does not know what he is doing. He does not know if his fans are cheering or booing. He is calm with everybody but with himself, he is family feuding. He is trying to get where he thinks he should be. He is trying to make his dreams his reality. He thinks he has a long way to go to reach his destiny. Sometimes, he feels dead like "Elvis Presley". He is trying to get ahead in life like "Monica Lewinski". He is short of breath and choking up like the old "Dirk Nowitzki". Every door he goes through seems to be the same. He tries his best to maintain. So many things stay on his brain. He did it and admits it but can't explain. He tries to get up but keeps falling like rain. He has love ones that are locked away. He doesn't keep in touch like he should but thinks about them every day. They say, "the child comes back after he or she goes astray". He not even 33 years old and his hair has turned gray. He is a grown man that acts like he has time to play. He wonders if anyone listens when he pray. He is so confused and does not know which way to go. He wants to win the race but only seems to "place or show". He seems to be getting smaller when he is really trying to grow. Like "R Kelly", he got some things he wants to keep on the "down low". He is mixed with mostly "bro". This guy is really confused. He prepares himself for good and bad news. Some people don't think he moves fast enough. They are at 4, while he is still at 2. Others think he ought to slow down and find something else to do. They even tell him, "this isn't working for you". He sees a bunch of people but only remembers a few. He is trying to "come up" but keeps getting pulled down. He has a smile but attracts so many frowns. Like the "$1.00" sign on the "Price is Right", he is trying to make it come back around. He is trying to reach the stars but can't seem to get off the ground. His shoulders are heavy like tons, bricks, and pounds. He needs a vacation. He needs to change towns. Maybe his confusion will eventually end. Maybe he will live right and no longer sin. Hopefully, he will recognize the difference between foes and friends. Maybe he will save his money and no longer spend. Make sure you pray for "Mr. Confused" because he is really trying to figure out what he needs to do.

Have you ever been on your last chance to get it right? You didn't know it was your last chance but it felt like it. Many times in your life, you let opportunity slip away. We must lose the phrases of, should have, I wish I had, and I could have done that. You must come into the now and do what has to be done, now. Your excuses will not ever get the task done so stop wasting your breath and wasting peoples' time listening to your negative excuses. You influence people by whatever you say.

This is for you and you only. This is for those times that you get lonely. This is for you when there is no shoulder to lean on. This is for you when no one seems to call your telephone. This is for you when you start to miss home. This is for you when you wish you could be a kid again and not be grown. This is for you when you get stressed out and don't know what your dreams are about. I know you get tired of hearing people scream and shout. I know it is hard to stay on a positive route. You have to handle your business and stop blaming others for your lack of faith. You must be ready to fight every single day. I know at times, your back is against the wall and it is hard to hold your head up and walk tall. I know "money get funny" and you can't seem to "ball". At times we want to break our own personal rules and laws. The bills seem to fall behind and make us think that we are loosing our mind. Life's uphill journeys have very steep inclines. Believe in yourself and everything will be fine. Always thank God, "The True Lord". You can win life's game. All you have to do is score. The "All Mighty" is going to help play defense on the floor. You have to use what you have before God will bless you with more. "The Nameless One" blesses you with whatever you ask for. That is why you have to watch your everyday speech and thoughts because God does not ignore. Be cautious of the people you let through your door. With positive situations, always explore. It is totally up to you, so make it do what it do.

In February of 1999, my cousin, "A-Ray" gave my oldest brother, "Ra Tem" and I an opportunity to have our own business so we opened "V I P Shoe Shine & Grocery". We were dropped into the "jungle" (hood) and we went at it. We didn't have all the tools we needed like money but that was no excuse. We had to use what we had. Our building was a condemned building initially until we took it from there. There were no doors. There was a hole in the ceiling in the back of the shop. There was no bathroom. (I used to have to go to a tree in the back or walk up the street to the YMCA for number 2). We were in a shopping center front but you could walk through the walls because there was only a frame left. I remember "Shorty" (a neighborhood walker) taking some old shelves out of another condemned building to give us our first candy racks. I remember the holes in the floor helped us design how we would decorate our establishment because all shelves had to cover up all holes. We even didn't have lights at first so we used "God's Sun". The customers didn't know because we kept batteries in the radio to make sure we had sounds when they came in. (If you hear sounds, you assume that there must be electricity). We kept cold drinks in an ice chest for sale. I bring this story up because we didn't sit around and wait for some magic to fall out of the sky. We did call on God to help guide us and give us strength. Then we did what God requires us to do and that is to get busy. We put it together piece by piece, door by door, wall by wall, and floor by floor. To get our floor started, we bought one piece of plywood and nailed it down to the floor. That one piece stayed there for about six months and then we added one more at a time. The next thing you know; my friend, "Brant Hudson" (R. I. P.) went to a church that was ready to renovate their church floor with ceramic tile. They donated their extra tile to our store which was enough to cover the whole store. My point is that you must put energy into whatever situation that you want to happen and God will help you if you help yourself. One piece at a time always completes the puzzle.

Know that, if you work toward completing the puzzle, it always makes you better. You have to know like "The Adam's Family knows Uncle Fester". You have to know like God knows weather and birds know feathers. You have to know like "Floyd knows Mayweather" and cheese knows cheddar. Know like Billy's Boot and Heel Repair shop knows leather and the dictionary knows "Webster". You have to know like cows know heifers, like Texas maps know "Keller", like tights know high steppers, and like intelligence knows clever. You have to know like trying to achieve knows endeavor and like "Locklear knows Heather". Know you have to get better like alphabets know letters and like miserable people know never. You have to know like the church knows their "Reverend". Know it like original knows trend setters and "Paparatis Wine Room" knows wine testers. Know it like the stock market knows investors. See, I know I've got to get better. I just need to figure out what I am waiting on. It is someone to tell me over the telephone. Do I need to see a text or hear a ring tone? Moving forward is the only way to get into the end zone. I need to admit it when I'm wrong and stop acting like I'm so "holy" just because I'm in the church choir singing songs. I need to leave these drinks alone and don't "front" on me because most of you all get "stoned". When I am weak, I need to be strong. I need to realize that I do not have long. I need to grow up because I am grown. My destiny should no longer be prolonged. I must keep God on my dome. I must continue to move right along and stop digging up the same old bones. I have to get away from these "zones". I need to hear a different station in my head phones and stay away from "Cheech and Chong". I have to stay away from bets and loans. It is my own cover that has been blown. "Heaven and hell" is the choice I must make right here and right now at home.

You have to make yourself better people. It takes praying, meditating, exercising, and eating right. No one wants to hear all of that crying you are doing. I finally stop complaining by realizing how many times I had to hear my own sad stories over and over. I would tell my sad story to one person and then the next person and so on. I realized that they only heard my story once but I had to keep hearing it over and over again. I got tired of hearing myself. I was able to hear how sorry I was being. I had to see about myself. Like "Michael Jackson" said, "I had to look at the man in the mirror". I am the only one that can make that change. If you are not getting better, you are getting worse. Being in neutral all the time just because you want to play it safe, does not make any progress. You are a sitting duck just waiting to be hit. You better put that gear in drive and push the gas on your life. The only thing you can do in neutral is, eventually run out of gas. You are the driver. The wheel is in your hand. Drive, driver.

Chapter 5

I'm Doing Me Right Now

I'm doing me right now. I do not have time for your problems. You are the only person that can solve them. I got some things that I need to take care of. To God, I have not shown enough love. I am coming out of my comfort zone and taking my phone off of roam. I am ready to answer like, "hello". I am ready to stop staying low. Like a volcano, I am ready to blow. To the internet is where I must take my show. Why should I stay local when I can reach foreign places like "Tokyo"? I am now going with the better ratio. I have books that I must work on. I got so much work to do that I need to be cloned. Who is going to help me when it is time to pay for my lights? I don't mind working grave yard. I will work all night and open my shop bright and early. I have to work a little harder and collect like "Mr. Ferley". My time has become so much more valuable. Things that I have allowed are no longer allowable. My demands are not negotiable. I know that my goals are attainable. Anything I set my mind to is gainful. I will always give God the credit. I will not be shameful. I am not just volunteering. I am also for hire. I can do it all. What do you desire? Do not be mad at me for trying to better myself. You can't be mad at God for giving me help! I know, keeping God 1st is the only way it will work. I have to know even when it hurts. Well anyway, I am doing me right now and if that offends you, you will get over it some day and somehow.

Don't be mad at me for doing me. You should be doing you. I am the only one that can do me and you are the only one that can do you. You can admire other people but you can only be yourself. Stop trying to be like other people and be who you are supposed to be. You are the greatest person you should know. If you goggled yourself on life's computer, would it be blank? Define yourself. Know who you are and what you are about.

I will make today the best day I ever had. My mind sees a great day before the day I have. If tomorrow comes, it will be the best I ever had. I have 24 hours. I don't have time to drag. Today, I will be more positive than ever before. Today I will win the game. I have to do more than just score. If you tell me that it can't be done, I will ignore. Tomorrow might not come so; I must live like, after this day, there are no more. I have so much business to handle. I have no fear. Problems, I will dismantle. I am trying to stay on top like the feet in "Passion of Christ" sandals. I'm hot like a "Texas dope phene" this summer wearing 3 flannels. There are only 60 seconds in this 1 minute. I need to create my own history before someone else tries to spin it. I have to stay strong and never quit it. Thank you Lord for waking me up this morning. I am thankful for every stretch and for yawning. Today will be exciting. It will not be boring. These breaths I breathe are not mine. I am only borrowing. Today, I must push on even if I am tired. I have to move forward because at any time, my life could be expired. I am my own boss. I have been hired. Today, I must hand out business cards and flyers. Today, I must read some truth. I have to exercise because I am growing older in my youth. I have to go to this business expo and get me a vendors' booth. I must advertise. This is what I must do. I need a spark in my life like electricity. I basically have to get busy. I have to keep going even if I feel sick and queasy. I am trying to move up past "Tom, Helen, George, and Wheezy". I have to sell me some soda water. I have to trade services. I have to barter. Most importantly, I must always pray to the "Mother and Father". I can either ride the bench or be a starter. I can walk, ride the bus, drive or fly the plane. No matter what today brings, I only have myself to blame. I have to make sure I always have a positive target when I aim. I have to keep pushing like muscles that strain. I have to be a good example to children and to those that are grown. I can stay under the bridge or get me a home. I don't want to do like a c. d. and keep repeating the same old song. Today is better than yesterday and you can't convince me that I am wrong. Today is the best day I have ever had. This should also be your best day. Let go of all the thoughts that are bad.

You have to make this day better because this is the only one that you have. You are not guaranteed any more days. Too often, the day passes us by and we did not get any of our business taken care of. Often times, the day passes by and we can't recall what we have done for the day. This is usually because we have not done anything. If you don't get off of your butt, you will be one of those people taking talents with you to your grave. That is selfish. God gave you those talents for a reason. You will have stories about what you should have done. You are the only one that can make your day good or bad.

What do you choose?

I have to keep going. My failures are not failures. They are only lessons showing. I have a purpose on this Earth that was decided before "Susan" ever gave me birth. I have some major business to take care of. I have to keep going when it seems like no one shows me any love. I have to keep going even when they don't believe in me. I have to keep going if I want to be all I can be. It is up to me to make a change. If I don't change, things will stay the same. I am the only person that can make me rise. Lord, I ask that you help keep me wise. Make me aware of my true enemies and give me the protection that I need. You have blessed humans so much in so many ways. I thank you for all of my hours and all of my days. I have to keep going even when others decide to stop. I have to keep going or sit, mildew, and rot. When I leave, I want my purpose to have been fulfilled and I have to keep in mind that all deals are not good deals. With myself, I have to keep it real. One day, I hope you feel what I feel.

I know we run into brick walls sometimes. I know people trip us up and stab us in the back. They step on our shoes and cut us off on the freeway. If you accidentally cut them off, you get to lip read their curse words. People look at you in your face and lie very good. People ignore you sometimes and wish the worse for you. It does not matter. You need to stop letting people affect you in negative ways. You literally have to start eliminating people out of your life. When you pray and mediate, stop letting their picture enter your thoughts. Stop putting energy into people that mean you no good. Replace one thought with a greater thought. You can't keep putting energy into things that you really do not want. If you keep people or things that you do not want on your mind, you still attract them or it to you. They will not stay away because you keep them in your thoughts. Your mind is a gigantic magnet. Be careful of what you attract to yourself.

This reminds me of a story when I was in college at "Texas Southern University". I was easily influenced and in turn became the ring leader of the situation. My freshman year, I stayed on campus in a dorm called "Bolton Hall". Across the parking lot was the closed down female dorm and I do not remember what the name of it was. It may have been about 1:00 in the morning on a night that I should have been sleep because I had class later that morning. A great buddy of mine noticed a window that was open at the girls' dorm and he said, "I bet you won't go in there". I was a betting nut in those days. I took that bet with no money. That is why I called myself a nut. There was so much at stake and nothing to gain in this bet. I climbed in the window; and to my amazement, I was in dorm room paradise. All the rooms were fully furnished including the hall ways and the lobby area. I went and opened the door to let my buddy in. I carried a nice polished wood coffee table back with me across the parking lot. He grabbed him a mattress. When I saw that, I said, "man, I got to come back and get me a couple of those". We had closed the door that automatically locks so I had to go through the window again. There goes the young nut in me again but this time I woke my room mate up and

51

some other fellow freshman nuts. We left the door propped open this time. We made about three or four trips over there and had our rooms sitting real nice like a dorm room should be. The fact that we had four mattresses on our beds did not help cover anything up. Well anyway, "Rev" came and unlocked our door about 9:00 that morning. "Rev" was the R.A. (residential assistant). I assume that at one point in his life, he may have even preached a message or two. "Rev" had been up watching us from the very beginning. He pointed me out as the guy that went in the window. I was easily noticed because I had an afro back then. Now, there are thousands of students going back and forth across the "yard" (campus). He made all 7 or 8 of us carry everything back in front of everybody. We looked like a line of ants taking stuff back to the ant hill. His attempt was to embarrass us and it worked. We also had to go to the student court for this situation. (Court has a story of its own too, lol) I could have been a good influence but I choose otherwise. Stay away from people that want you to join them in doing wrong. You know what is wrong and right. Don't fall for it. In reality, we could have been charged for theft. If you decide to be the ring leader, lead the right way. Don't do like I did.

That was my younger years. Now I have grown up. I heard a great speaker say, "you can't get what you need where you are or you would have it." You must be the most positive person you know. The most positive person I know is me. To be more positive than me, I can't let you be and please don't take that negatively. Let me tell you so you can see it how I see. If I am supposed to be in God's image, there is no reason to do anything different. The "Nameless One" is the "coldest" spoken word artist I know. I am in God's image, so I have to be "Phroze". You are what you think. We are all part of a chain that links. My thoughts become my reality. I have to let my dreams live so they will not become a fatality. Whatever the outcome, I am the blame. My original "Mother and Father" are named God if you must know their name. I am one of God's sons. Some say "Jesus" was the only one. Others say, "it's the bright and morning Sun". Whatever you believe, what's done is done. I only want to associate with positive people, please. I don't have time for tricks up sleeves. Get "Heaven on Earth" in case some of these stories are just "tall tales". I don't mind trying again if I fail. I have to create my environment. I love life and I am not looking for retirement. I have to talk positive to myself before anyone else does. I have to love myself before I can give you any love. Being the best me is the only way I can be the best to you and the same needs to go for you too. You have to be the best that you can. God gave choices to woman and man. What do you choose? Do you choose to be led by the evening news? I am just asking. You don't really have to answer. Stop looking at everyone else's pictures and get your own camera. Go see stuff for yourself. Stop being stingy with help. Didn't anyone ever teach you to share? Didn't someone teach you to care? Well anyway, the most positive person I know is "Phroze" and you should be the most positive person you know.

It is unhealthy to be mad and sad all the time. You waste so much energy that can go toward positive moments in your life. The person that always complains to you always has something to complain about. Don't take it personal and get away from them as fast as possible. However, a person is with you is how they are with others so value first appearances. Trust your instincts. You always have to do what is best for you but don't hurt others in the process. You will never please everybody. Everybody will not please you. Just keep it moving because you have so much more life to live.

It is literally time to make things happen. Some things are serious but you are still laughing. I am ready to take my talent to the next level. I have more than one option. I actually have several. I'm talking about doing some world trade type stuff and that is with no bluff. I need to make sure I am serving God's purpose. I am through playing with you all like I am part of a circus. Nothing is stopping me like a handicap. I am ready to take the top off of the salary cap. I am ready to really let my "paper stack" and I am through putting out negative things back to back. Nothing but positive things shall come from my voice. I can stay in a rut but to grow is my choice. You all are really not ready for me. Just give me a little time and you will see. There is more to it in this life I live. I am ready to receive after I give. I am ready for you to look me up on w w w dot. I have too much inside me to stay in this one spot. I am ready to go in "hot pursuit" like a "Dukes of Hazard cop". I am ready to ignore you all that "knock". I no longer hear you when you mock. Don't say, I am part of the lost sheep because they are the dumbest flock. "Coach God" put me in the game but I have taken the wrong shots. I must always give it all I got. I must continue. There is no reason to stop.

My father sent me a text that read, "I heard that the secret to long life is to not work for other people". When I was at the "modern day slave plantation" (the job) the other day, I read a quote that said, "the only time success comes before work is in the dictionary". I really like both of those quotes. I have worked hard for other people with a little pay so I learned to do work hard for myself. The catch is this though. When you get serious about your own business, many of your friends and family still will not take you that serious. You have to let them know from the beginning. If they think you are being "shady", don't care. When you work for someone, everybody respects that. If you can't have phone calls at work, they don't call. They don't ask for rides because they know you are on the clock. You make sure you get to work on time too even if that means taking a chance with every-body's life because you need to drive like a "bat out of hell". You can't be late anymore. When you open your own business, people will ask you to close down for a while because they need a ride. Friends come by and say they want to help; however, it becomes more of a hang out for them. People love to give suggestions on how you should run eve-rything but don't offer a dime to help implement their ideas. Like "Baba Amin" said, "criticism is welcomed but examples are preferred". Some are just sitting and waiting for your down fall. I have family that would come by the shop but would never spend a dime with me. They want you to just give them something for free. They don't even ask for credit. I guess they forgot that, "Gimme got his arm broke for messing with his kin folks". Following your visions and dreams can be a lonely world but sometimes in life you need to be alone to accomplish what needs to be done.

What others have accomplished, I can too. To myself, I have to stay true. I have been blessed with the same abilities. I have the same possibilities. I have full coverage, not just liability. I can knock out my trials undisputedly. I have to hit the right notes like melodies. People need to come together instead of staying separately. This is my opinion personally. I am pushing toward success desperately. I have to get it drastically. I have to join positive teams like a faculty. Keep a steady pace and pick it up gradually. I have to master my goals like mastery. Too many times, I have acted like success is nasty. I have to stay tough and not break like glassy. It has to happen now. It has to be presently. Keep in mind that life is always testy. You have to change some things up like when white milk is mixed with "Nestle".

No one is greater than anyone else. If has been done, it can be done again. If it has not been done, it can still be done. It is totally up to you. It takes work, patience, and trusting the God that is with you every day. Learn from others examples, even those that have failed. Look at their failures so you will know what not to do. Ask those whom are already doing what you want to do for advice. People love to tell their, "how I made it stories". Use their lessons in life for your own lessons in life. You can save yourself so much time and pain.

If you are hanging with 9 broke friends, there is a great chance that you will become number 10. All you talk about is how bad your bills are and how you do not have a car. You always talk about not being able to pay your rent. Your complaints never seem to quit. Just because you do not have money does not give you the right to cuss out the kids. The hole, you do not climb out of. The hole, you dig. They told you how bad they day was and your response was, "I feel ya, shoot". Tighten your circle up. It's too loose and your circle might be lonely. Some do not want you to succeed. They "fronting". They are really phony. You can't continue to entertain broke if you want to be rich. Feelings may get hurt but it is still time to switch. Misery does love company but success does too. Before you can love others, you have to love you. Make it do what it do, baby. Make it do. If they want to sit on the porch and get "throwed" all day, let them do that. Let them have their way but if you want change, point the finger at yourself. When you don't have money, it is hard to help. At the end of your life, only you will get the blame. Broke folks hang with broke folks and the rich do the same. Don't become the 10th broke friend and with that being said, this chapter comes to an end.

Chapter 6

Choose Your Words Carefully

While you are stuck in the past, the rest of the world is still going. When you stay in the past, you stop yourself from growing. When you stay in the past, you may miss out on certain opportunities. All you can do is live in the present is the reality. The past can never ever be changed. No matter how much you may want it to, the past will not be rearranged. Just stay or get strong and maintain. There is no reason to waste energy on your past pain. Just pray to the "Powers" that make the mountains, valleys, and plains. The past is gone like evaporated rain. Live in the present and plan for the future. Live here and now like the song by "Luther". The past may have been bumpy but it is up to you to make it smoother. Measure all your options like a measuring tape ruler. What's done is done and what you do now shall eventually be done. You can stay miserable or enjoy life and have some fun. Be thankful that you have a past to learn from. Some died before they were even 21. Hold your head up and stop looking at the floor. You know what is on the other side but you keep going through the same door. Stay positive and be careful because sometimes we crash. Handle your business now because you will be old in a flash. While you are stuck in the past, no one is waiting on you. You already know the outcomes of your past. You need no clues. Plan for your future and let old news remain old news. You have choices, so what do you choose? While you are stuck in the past, the rest of the world is still going. When you stay in the past, you stop yourself from growing.

Let the past go people. Stop putting energy into old negative stuff. When you bring it up or think about it, you keep bringing it back to life. You will find yourself going through the same thing again and won't understand why. It is because you never shut up about it. The new people you meet in life don't have to be like the old people. They keep being like the old people and you keep having the same situations in your life because you continue to feed it by giving it energy with your words and thoughts. Watch your thoughts and watch what you say.

Watch what you say because your thoughts and words always manifest. That is why you have to control them both. If you say you are doing badly, then you are. If you say you are doing well, then you are. We don't have bad days' only bad moments so stop saying that you are having a bad day. If you are having a bad moment, change the moment. Quit crying. Quit complaining. You bring forth sickness when you say, "I think I am getting sick". We also need to stop talking crazy to our children. They believe most of the things we say so when you call them stupid or tell them to stop acting so dumb, they start to believe they are stupid and dumb, especially if they hear the same thing at school every day. They don't correct other people because they hear the same things from their parents all the time. Your child is a "terrible two" because you keep calling them that and letting other people call them that. People ask you how you are doing and you respond, "I'm doing bad. I'm broke as a joke. My money funny. If someone tried to rob me, they would just be practicing" and you wonder why you stay broke. If we are really in God's Image, we are supposed to be speaking great things into existence, anyway. Choose your words carefully.

You have to watch your words but also be cautious of the things you hear. You don't have to believe what everybody say. Only believe God when you meditate and pray. They tell us only what they want us to know. Think about it. Television is a form of entertainment; therefore, the news is also a show. I need to see the parts that they cut out. I need to hear about things that no one else hears about. America found Bin Laden but some think we have been lied to. Some wonder if his character was even true. Do we know the true stories about those twin towers? Was there a bill on the floor that some wanted to devour? If they really wanted to stop this "drug rage", it would be as simple as turning a page; but think about it, that would cut off the maximum wage. Don't listen to them. You are the "star" of your life on stage. They say that when you dig deep, you will find that the government owes you back pay for being arrested because you were kidnapped and held for ransom. On another note; children, there is no "Santa Clause or Rudolph" and I do not apologize parents because you have your children lost. We even have "Easter Bunnies" laying eggs. Can we give the chicken its credit since they really come from between their legs? Stop having your children learn what's not true. All I ever want to do is bring truth. Don't tell me to turn on that news to see that negative mess. I see enough of that in my back yard and right in front of my chest. America will praise you until you get to certain levels. Then their evil spirit will treat you as a devil. They don't want us to dig deep like shovels. I don't believe everything I hear. I refuse to settle. The weather man will tell you that there is a 20% chance of rain on the forecast but why not tell me, "it's an 80% chance of sun shine is what I ask. They have us so brain washed that we think it is o.k. for the police to harass. Some people are literally out to make you look like an a#*. Don't believe everything that is on display. You will get yourself in trouble believing everything that people say. Always seek the truth. See past the facade and all the bull. Listening to the wrong thing will have you falling like a two leg stool but you can do what you want to do. Whatever decision you make, don't say that I didn't warn you.

We have been trained to believe whatever the media reports to us. We act like they really want us to know the truth. They want us to know what they want us to know. Once we hear or see the news, we run out and spread it for them. We even give our opinion of it and "juice it up" a little bit. People will look at you in your eyes and lie like they really telling the truth. Don't take it personal. If they are lying to you, they probably lie on a regular basis. They lie all day long to whomever they are talking to. Get away from these people. You know who they are and if you are this person, you need to change.

Don't believe everything they tell you. You make it too easy for them. They know what to do. They know what to feed you. You eat whatever they throw out. That is "slave food" that they are putting in your mouth. Whatever they report, you believe. You work for the media too because you spread the news like a disease. "Did you watch the news last night? Such and Such had a fight. He was cheating on his wife; not with Michelle, but with Mike. They robbed a bank and got away". That is the news for today but tomorrow they got something new. "You know his wife was cheating too and they shot them fools that robbed that bank. They tried to do it again but the car would not crank. Learn how to discern things that you hear. The media will have you running around hear living in fear. They will have you hating people that you never met. Just be aware because they will never quit.

Don't let these folks drive you crazy. Just because they say it was gang related, does not mean that it was. Just because they say it was a drug deal gone bad, does not mean it really was. Just because they tell you something about a celebrity does not mean it is true. They report more opinions than facts. They will report a double homicide and suicide but they could be protecting somebody that is not in the picture (like a police for example). They portray certain people in certain ways through movies and television shows. For example,

"Denzel Washington" has done so many great movies but did not get his "Oscar" award until he did the negative movie, "Training Day". It is not a surprise that, "Empire" is one of the number one shows. It promotes the agenda. Just be careful of what you hear and see and be extra careful of what you repeat.

A man, who controls his mouth, is a man of character. Character is defined as personality or moral strength. To control your tongue is truly a gift. There is no reason to stoop to other people's low levels. When people look at you, they should not see a devil. Why are you always frowning up? You should really let those wrinkles settle. Someone just cursed you out so now you feel it is your turn. Now, you are thirsty. You got them back so good that your mouth burns. You are steady letting negative people get on your nerves. Is it God or man? Which one do you serve? Walk a straight line. Don't let the enemy make you curve. Before you speak, think about your words. You don't have to prove anything to anybody. The only one you have to answer to is the "All Mighty". Stop letting people run you hot like bacon that you fry and some of you all ought to hear yourselves when you get drunk and high. Some of you all talk crazy and are sober all day long. Your mouth stays open like an opera singer who sings songs. You should not even talk if your information is wrong. Actions have always spoken louder than words. Your mouth moves faster than the wings on a bird. You should really try to control your tongue. This is how you become positive daughters and sons. It is up to you to make your aura glow. It is not wise to be a star in every show because sometimes the star gets shot and has to go. You should really hear yourself when you talk. This might change the path that you walk. Just listen to how you really sound and you might start to see why people hate for you to come around. Negative thoughts and words should be lost and never found.

Always remember that people are listening to you. You might not know it but they are, especially children. A lot of people that hear you try to avoid you because they don't want to be around anything that sounds that bad. Like I said, "one important thing to remember is that you have to hear all of your negative stories over and over again every time you are talking to someone else". You may not realize it but it is effecting your life, over and over again. Be careful with your thoughts and your words.

Chapter 7

All You Have Is Today

Tomorrow is dead until tomorrow. From God; all days are borrowed, so use the one you have today. Once tomorrow is here, you can forget yesterday because days come and go. Days are laid out in a row. You can only live them one at a time. Whatever you seek, you will find. You are in control of how your days unfold. You are living your story. It is not just being told. Whatever you think comes to past. Live everyday like it is your last. There is always work to be done. Always strive to be number one. Stay "kingdom and queendom minded" because we are great kings and queens. Save tomorrows thoughts for your dreams. Today is all you have and all you need. Every day, we plant seeds. Some people know what I mean. Tomorrow is dead until tomorrow. I thank God for all these days that I borrow.

Live in the here and now. I am not saying don't plan for the future but take full advantage of what you have now. Handle today's moments while you have the chance. There is no time to waste. Stop believing that you have to wait on somebody else to validate you. Validate yourself. You don't need their approval. Approve yourself. Use what you have. God gave the Earth to you so you are already approved. As long as you keep saying what you are going to do, you will be forever just talking about going to do it. Change your speech to say,

"I am doing it (whatever it is) now.

There is always another battle to face after you have won. Go ahead and finish what you have begun. Accept whatever has to be done. God is always in control so just move right along. Become an entrepreneur even if that means you have to work late. You can only go with the now. You can't change yesterday. All you have is today. My jobs have never paid me enough wages. As a matter of fact, I haven't paid myself enough wage. I have to take care of my business because there is no time to play and "just say no" like in the fifth grade. How many times will I take a lost before I realize that I am not getting paid? It is some things going on with me that I can't write down. If I have to, I will move around because my circle can't have any spaces. It has to be tight. I thank God that I can "spit" what I write. I must always use my "dome". I must work hard to have a happier home. I can't get my spirit right if I keep doing wrong. It is not easy being grown. I am trying to make my "paper long". We need our own. It can be done without their loans. Give me some time alone, please. Praying does not have to be on your knees. What is my next step? When will I get some rest? Be careful of what you do because memories do stick. The only way to really lose, is to quit. Always keep God in your house. You must work and not be "potatoes on the couch". Life is too short to waste. I am not trying to prove anything but I do rest my case.

You have to make your situation better. I understand that

some love to work for other people and that is o.k. I actually am excited to one day give you a job. If you are working for someone, make sure you are at least doing what you enjoy and I do understand that sometimes you may have to do what you do not want to do to get to where you want to be. My suggestion to everyone else is to, do your best to work for yourself. At the same time, be ready and willing to train others how to run your business. You find more success when you can be away and your business still runs smoothly. You have to see your vision and stick to it no matter what. You will always have obstacles but it is not what happens to you. It is always how you react to what has happened or is happening to you. We have been trained to go to school so we can get a good job. Others are taught to go to school and learn to open their own business, their own practice, or their own office. If they can do it, you can too. Create your own reality people. Get up and get busy.

It might not always be wise to finish what you begin. All stories eventually see an end so I need to take care of the in between. These are mine. They are not your dreams. There are certain goals that I have to set and there are certain checks that I have to get so excuse me if I've stepped on your shoes. That tends to happen to people that never make moves. I don't mean any disrespect at all but you either ride bench or you "ball". When you try to stop me, I still go. I'm on 24 hours. Others are just a late night show. God knows I am trying to get it right. God knows I am "young and restless" and that I want to follow the "guiding light". Sometimes it feels like I have been here before. Thank you "Big Brant" for helping with the store. May you rest in peace and help keep me in line. I have to be ready when it is my time. This, I really can't ignore. I have to "wake up and stop the snore". I have to just do it and stop the crying. Lord, help me see because I must be blind. My mama's new heart almost gave me a heart attack. I speak truth so I speak facts. I can't stand "smile in your face rats". I wish my kin folk was not smoking crack. I used to be a "mack". I think I am growing up and I am not scared to say that. I try not to "strike out when I bat". Creating my "Heaven" is now a lot more important than trying to let my "money stack". I don't need trophies on my rack. I need my train to jump to the other track. I am a spoken word artist. Some think, I rap. Before I leave, I hope to get to visit the whole map because I think there is a lot more out there than where I am at. I know that it is all up to me. I am the only one that decides what I will truly be.

It is totally up to you to be what you are supposed to be. If you don't, that is the wrong decision that you are making in your life. Things happen in our lives. When will you accept that? You must stay in balance. When things don't go your way, stop getting "out of wack". Stop beating yourself up all the time. That never has and it never will change things. When you come across hard times, don't get too down and when things are going great, don't get too high. Don't get me wrong. Enjoy the moment to the fullest but remember, we all eventually have to come back. Life is full of ups and downs. Stay balanced.

An old friend called and asked what I was up to. My response was, "I'm just trying to stay true". I am just like "Jesus of the bible" in one way because I'm out here in these streets. I desire to reach everyone, not just 2 or 3. I told him I was out here trying to get rich and prosperous because there is a difference. I am out here trying to get wealthy. I am trying to get my family spiritually, mentally, and physically healthy. He wanted to know what I was up to. I told him that I was getting older in my youth. I told him I needed to exercise and like dough, "I was trying to rise". I'm trying to be a better example. I am trying to be "the real deal", not just a sample. I've been shining boots and zappattos. I told him, I still have shows that I host. I am trying to make it happen from coast to coast. I am different so I never try to be like most. I am an entrepreneur and I work a job. If I keep working on mine, I eventually won't have to report to "Richard, Ashley, or Bob".

I hope you can understand what I am saying. I am a grown man. I don't have time to be playing. It is time for me to get back in the studio. Every day, I must grow. I am "bleeding these streets" and becoming an author, ya dig. He asked what I was up to. I told him I was trying to make a kid. The "good book" reads to be "fruitful. I made it to my thirties but I still feel so youthful. I am just trying to make it happen. I keep telling them that I am a "spoken word artist". I don't be rapping. I told him that I was trying to make a "hundred dollars out of 15 cents". I told him I was working so I could pay my mortgage, bills, and rent. I am trying to put food on my family's table. I am trying to get the satellite back on and stop "boot legging" cable. I am trying to take charge. I want more than a one car garage. I am trying to move from the house to the castle. I am trying to graduate life and I don't need a tassel. He asked what I was up to. I said, "something man". From this day forward, I will never say nothing again.

I don't have any time to waste. I must do what has to be done today. I must always keep myself busy. I don't plan on going to my grave with my business unfinished. I like being ahead of my time. I like doing what others are scared to do. I have to believe in me. That is why I am finally doing this book. I have to take care of my business because no one else can do it for me. Successful people don't stop. They always strive for more success, ya dig.

Chapter 8

It Is Time For Me To Grow

Never fear. The "sixth man" is here. I am good to give 100%. I come in to play offence and defense. I can handle the pressure. I can take a hit. I am the "sixth man", right off the bench. I come in adding life. I did not come to lynch. This is not a dream. Your arm does not need to be pinched. The championship game must be clinched. We all need each other to win the game. I make shots from short and long range. Many moments in life force you to change. Sometimes, your plans have to rearrange. I need the money, not the fame. I come to help pick up the team like a crane. I help keep everyone calm. There is no reason to go insane. I make sense out of situations that you may find strange. God is always my teams' coach and I am too serious for it to be a joke. I am just following the game plan so from God, I take notes. My life is in these words that I wrote. You must stay strong even when you feel like you can't cope. All I am trying to do in life is rise to the top like smoke. Keep in mind that we are riding in the same boat. I tell coach that I can do it when others have told the coach, "no". I will not disappoint God when God puts me in. All I know how to do is, try to win. I am o.k. with being the "sixth man" off the bench. All I know; is that, I promise to give 100%.

God created a team of people. God did not just make you and I. The "Nameless One" designed us to work together. That is what we must do. This is the only way we can be a success. We think we are doing this thing on our own. There is no way possible. There is too much work to be done to do it by yourself. Many times on this journey, you may think that you do not get the credit that you deserve. Keep going anyway. Know that your "pay off" is bigger than any recognition a person could ever give you. Always see past the physical. Look deep inside yourself because that is where you truly find God. Don't be average. You must always strive to be great for the sake of the whole team. Also remember that you may have to change your team up because there is a such thing as being on the wrong team. Choose your teams wisely. You are always a "free agent".

Stop staying so loyal to things that don't work. Let some people go even though it hurts. To your goals in life, you must assert. You must put in effort while you are still on top of dirt. Second place is not remembered, only first. You must take the game in your own hands like "Jordan, Magic, or Dirk". Stop asking for pants when you know you need a shirt. Wake up people. Please don't be a jerk. You are too loyal to those that are not loyal. Always keep in mind that you are royal. If you sit out too long, you will "spoil". Finish the job and wrap it up like foil. If it is not helping the community and generating dividends, there is no reason for you to even step in. You have to stay positive and try not to sin. You should not be in the bleachers knowing that the race is about to begin. If you do not practice, there is no way you will ever win. You must have faith like the bible story of "Daniel in the Lion's Den". It is time to get our act together, woman and man.

Step out of your boundaries. Go ahead and expand. Stop being so loyal to things that don't work. In the end, it is only you that truly hurts.

You are practicing insanity if you keep doing the same thing and expecting different results. If it is not working, it is up to you to change your situation. Your time is so valuable. Stop wasting these God given moments. Use your energy to be positive. If it is not positive energy, it can only be negative. Stop letting negative influences, influence you. Drop all the "zeros" and get around heroes and she-roes.

Break away from destructive attitudes and negative influences. Maintain a positive attitude and manage your emotions. Stay focused. Always work on your personal growth. Professionals have coaches. Amateurs do not. Be a good student. Step out there, learn from your mistakes, and don't be afraid to start over as many times as you need to. If you don't put anything in, don't expect anything to come out. Don't be a grudge holder. Misery loves company and remember, success does too. Don't let their low self-esteem bring you down. Find you a new group, with their mind tuned into a positive station. If you keep hanging with negative people, you have a better chance to turn negative than you have in turning them positive because you are out numbered. The right people need to know that you can be counted on. Yesterday is gone, so leave it there. You have to live today and maybe even tomorrow.

It is time for me to grow; therefore, it is time for me to let some things and some people go. I need to let them go for real like they "zero" and I hate to say it but, some of these people are my "kin folks". They are doing things to me "on the low" and I think that they think that I do not know but I do. I really, really do. I know you are watching me but God is always watching you. I have to grow because I play too much. I admit that I have done some bad stuff. I can make it smooth but I must want to keep it rough. Am I trying to fool myself? Is it me that I am trying to bluff? I know that I have rhymes to write. I know that I must flip the switch to have light. I can no longer choose what it is wrong when I know what is right. I can never learn to fly the airplane if I never get past the bike. I know I have plenty of work to go record. There is always more to do so you will never hear me say that I'm bored. Whatever I want and need, I should be able to afford. I need to take care of my health a lot better because right now, I'm sore. All I know is that it is time for me to grow; therefore, there are some things and some people that I need to let go.

No matter what, your life's destiny is always up to you. You must take responsibility for your actions. Even though you may want to, you can't be a physical child again. It will really benefit you and I to grow up. Be the example that you are supposed to be for the next generations that are trying to grow up. They will follow whatever example you give them no matter if you are trying to or not. There comes a time when we must grow up. You were not put here to stay young. You are supposed to get old but it is totally up to you to make yourself grow.

Chapter 9

Stop Giving Major Time To Minor People

Some people are not trying to go where you are going, so why do you keep trying to take them? He keeps telling you "no" but you keep trying to take him. Make sure you know who you are marrying before you become husband and wife. Live yours and let them live their life. The "one" who loves misery, refuses to reach for higher heights. You can't mix wrong with right. Every time you say it will work, they totally disagree. You keep looking at them when you should look in the mirror at what your eyes see and everybody don't believe in the "'Big G". Some don't believe that God made the tree. Stop helping people bend the truth like elbows and knees. Strive to stay on top like the "fingers on top of Alicias' piano keys". Some people stay content in the rut they are in. It is hard to live right when you surround yourself with so much sin. A lot of the people you are trying to take don't even want you to begin. They wish that your road to success would eventually run into a dead end. Stay encouraged. You have to go until the end. In reality, everyone does not want you to win. They talk behind your back but in your face, they grin. Use your head and stop operating below the chin. Some people refuse to come out of their comfort zone. Some remain nuts like acorns. They will tell you anything and they know they are wrong. Be careful about who you let enter your home. Like I said, "you must use your dome". Those folks never have anything good to say when they call your cell phone. Some want to be the choir director but don't even know the songs. Every time you ask them to do something, they seem to whine and moan. Just know that you must let some go before God will allow you to move on.

You keep trying to give them rides but they keep telling you they are going the opposite way. Accept the fact that you are different like night and day. You are different like my "Uncle Paul and my Aunt Faye". You are different like being broke and getting paid. You are different like keep, sale, and trade. You are different like pre-school and the 12th grade. You are different like stream and spray. You are different like December and May. You are different like the English word "what" and the Spanish word, "que". You are so totally different like "Africa" and "The United States". All I am saying is, "why must you fall behind"? You need to stay in your lane and let them walk their own line. A lot of you all are trying to give people rides just because they are physically fine. You need 100% but you can't get there if you keep picking up those that really want to be left behind. See the person, instead of the material things that shine. Keep your mind right because whatever you seek, you shall find. Stay focused and stop letting negative people speak into your mind. They never pay you back but always want to borrow a dime. Let the people going the same way as them, pick them up. Drive yourself or walk. Stop hopping in and out of everybody's car or truck. Catch rides with positive people and stop riding with nuts. Weigh your options. Weigh your "ifs, ands, and buts". It is up to you to make your life "turn up". Sometimes, you need to leave your door shut. Go with your true feelings. Go with what you feel in your gut. You can't have the brick home if your mind set is always on shacks and huts. Every time you pick them up, you have to listen to their problems. They will not do anything for themselves. They want you to solve them. Stop letting people take you off of your road to success. It is up to you to past your own test. You do not have time to be playing with these people. Stop associating with the wrong crowd. With those you want to be like, you need to mingle. You have business to take care of and there is no time to waste so stop giving rides to people going the opposite way.

Learn discernment and choose the people for your life wisely. When you get that feeling of someone you meet that does not feel right, please trust your thoughts. That is the God in you telling you what to do. When you go against your own thoughts and deal with these people any way, you eventually have to pay for it one way or another. Discern, not only people but situations and everything else that tries to come into your life. You have already wasted so much time trying to get people to get in the car with you that do not really want your ride. Many times in life, you may have to ride solo until the God in you attracts what and who you need for your personal journey.

Stop giving major time to minor people. The whole day is gone and what have you done? Well, you partied all day and night so you did have fun. You "got full" and don't quite remember what happened last night. Don't let man bring you down. There is no reason to fight. Why are you riding coach when you should be on your personal jet flight? I mean, help me to really understand. You need to put your faith in God, not man. If you do it that way, God will send you the right people for your life. You are hanging with people that can't wait to stab you in the back with a knife. All day, you hang with people that find enjoyment in strife. Why are you so scared to "step out on water"? You are your team so you can't "ride the bench". You have to be a "starter".

At all times, pray and give 100% and stop spending so much time with people that bring you down like a gavel on the judge's bench. To minor people, you are giving major time. You can either prosper or remain behind. You know that you have business to take care of. Before you can do it for others, you have to show yourself some love. Try not to be a time waster. Try to be a lover and not a hater? You might not want to but you need to hear it. Take care of your mind, body, and spirit. Stop letting people throw you off track. It is totally up to you if you want to move from the front to the back. Do not be afraid to be that positive example. Instead of using your whole potential, you are just giving out samples. You are in the middle of the wilderness wearing sandals. Put your boots on and get ready to stomp. To get to the top of the mountain, you can't stay in the swamp. Remember that misery loves company and you can only blame yourself. Other people are not obligated to give you help. Stop giving major time to minor people. You have to save yourself and stop leaving it up to the preacher. You can prosper a lot more in the major league. It has already been planted. How will you grow your seed? If you involve God, God will send you the people that you need.

I am not saying that you should ignore those in need but if they don't want to help themselves, you are wasting your time. At the same time, you can't burn yourself out trying to make sure that everybody else's life is o.k. A lot of times; people will use you up, knowingly or unknowingly. They don't pay you back like they promised and now you can't afford to pay your bills. They move in and never help with the rent or any other bill. They need a ride everywhere but never have any gas money; even though, it takes way more than gas to run a car. These are only a few examples. If you keep saying yes to everyone all the time, you hurt both you and them. They tend to look at you as a God because you never say "no". You never give them a chance to really go and work on it or pray about it. At the same time, your business is not taken care of. You don't know what you will eat today or tomorrow. Sometimes, you have to learn how to show tough love and say, "no". This is the only way that both of you can grow.

Chapter 10

Inquiring Minds Want To Know

I have always wondered and questioned things that other people would never vocally question. I am not trying to prove anything to you. I am just forever learning my lesson. I just wonder about a few things, like the satellites that connect our phones that ring. I wonder why the penny is made of a different material than other coins like the dime and why it faces the opposite way when laid down in a line. I wonder if the police are a branch of the "klu klux klan" even though; on the squad, you can always find a black man. A casket has six sides and there are six pall barriers. You are buried six feet deep but don't let that scare us. The "three 6's" are a regular ritual practiced every week. Please, keep your cool. Stay humble and meek. I just wonder about a few things, like how I sometimes see reality before reality in my dreams. I also don't think that the root of all evil is currency. Could the root of all evil just be evil in reality and I wonder why things are so crazy politically? Will the final decision really have anything to do with the vote from me? I wonder about the people that are really behind certain drugs like crack and medicine to heal the stomach, head, and back. I wonder why we have been taught to not use herbs that are natural. They want us to pop their pill with side effects that can be fatal. I wonder why we should have to pay for electricity, gas, and water; when they really belong to the "Life Starter". They belong to the "God Father and Mother". I also noticed that someone purposely taught us to call each other b*tches and n*ggas instead of sisters and brothers. Why do we get immune to poverty? At the same time, the "system" makes you hungry which causes some to commit robbery. Why aren't certain things revealed to us like a "congress bill"? America stays at war even though the bible states, "thou shall not kill". We are taught that when we get to "Heaven", we will have wings that fly but birds already have wings and I just wonder why. If "Eve" ate a physical apple from the tree, why is o.k. to eat apples now? Please, just tell me. People in the bible followed physical present men but soon as we do, somebody is calling it sin. They want me to "down" my present physical leaders. Other than in the bible, can you prove that there was a "Mathew, Mark, Luke, or Jesus"? I am not saying that they didn't live. I just wish someone could show proof of what I was taught as a kid.

Why is the number 13 all over the back of the dollar and reads Latin words that translate to, "one world order"? In some buildings, there is not a thirteenth row. Images are given to us so we can move in the direction that someone else wants us to go. For example; I was given the images of slavery to stop me from becoming a king. I often wonder about the universe and things unseen. I also wonder why we believe any and every thing the doctor has to say. Some of us know that the body heals or kills by your thoughts and what it consumes every day. Someone is making billions of dollars off of medication. Once you change your mind, you change your situation. I try not to hate. I try to bring inspiration. Could the real meaning of imagination be to imagine a nation. I just wonder about a few things that no one else ever seems to vocally question. I am not trying to prove anything. I am just forever learning my lesson.

There are so many things that people really don't think about; like the fact that, you hurt yourself when you always fight and shout. Some jokes that are told are really a lie and if you haven't been to "Heaven or hell", how can you honestly tell me what it is like when I die? Why are "Debbie's devil cakes black and the angel cakes are white"? Many times, we choose wrong even when we know it is not right. I think that every grown person should own a gun based off the history that our government has done. Many say the "bible" is about the zodiac so is the "Son of God and Sun of God" the same and did God really destroy the Earth with rain? How did "Noah" keep the cold weather animals satisfied? I know you never thought about it but I always ask, "how and why". Even though the news reports news, it does not mean it is true news and why are the blues called the blues? What is it that they don't report to us every time they go into outer space? I wouldn't be surprised if folks were living in that outer place. When the politician says that they want to make the country better, what do they consider better and if God made everything good, is there really such a thing as bad weather? Who caused curse words to be understood? The one, who thinks that he can't, never could. There is a chance that man created aids so man has a cure for aids and because of greed, aids keeps them paid. Do you really have to go to jail to be in jail? Does success always come after you fail? Why do some not want to give credit to the people that built the pyramids and castles back then? They want me to believe that aliens did it and not, Africans. I am just putting a little on your mind. Always know that you can move ahead no matter how much they try to keep you behind.

I understand that I may never get all the answers to the things that I question. Most of my answers will not come because the majority of the people do not know the answers. We accept whatever we are fed. We have never questioned our teachers or preachers because we always assumed that whatever they were teaching had to be true. If a teacher gives the answers, you never go and verify that information. Why don't you, though? We need to take inchoative and do further research on the subjects that are presented to us. It is totally up to you to learn as much as you can. It is also up to you, to unlearn some things. Just because it is true to you, does not make it true. Only facts prove the truth.

Inquiring minds want to know. Let me tell you just in case you inquire. You must hit your target hard like "Sammy Sosa and Mark McGuire". Stay on the top. Stay hot like fire. Never quit the task. Never retire. It is very possible to have everything that you desire. Tell the truth because people can't stand a liar. Don't let man intimidate you. I don't care if his name is "Michael Myers". In success and prosperity, always push to go higher. Before you go to that place, look at the subliminal messages on that flyer. Take your life more serious.

Your life can't always be comedy like "Richard Pryor". Choose your possessions wisely because you are the buyer. Stay unified like one of those big church choirs. If you are giving up too much information; be careful, because they might tap your wire. Take care of your business before your life expires. Be careful because, some people try to trap you in their internet webs like spiders. Don't jump yet. You have to be a rider. You have to keep everything rolling like tires. Every day is a new day so every day, you have been hired. Stop letting stuff wear you down, like wet clothes that never made it to the dryer. Keep a firm grip on your life like vice grip pliers. Stop living in slavery. Once again, become great rulers and sires. You have decisions to make. What will you let your mind, inquire?

It is totally up to you. Your mind actually believes the way you are thinking. That is why you must purposely have positive thoughts. When the negative thoughts try to enter your brain, you have to hurry up and get rid of them. You can't let them hang out. The outcome of your life is from the thoughts you put into it. Your thoughts are like words that speak so loud that everything in the universe hears it and acts on it.

If you go there in the mind, you can go there in the body. Before you even got to the club, you thought about the party. You really hoped it would be "on fleek" tonight. You hated that person before the fight. I think of the words before I write. The artist pictures the future picture first. Before the choir could sing, they had to rehearse. If you don't believe it, you will not get it. The inside of your head should not sound like crickets. It should sound like positive thoughts. When you go into a store, you don't think free because you know stuff cost. You can't get any smarter if you continue to hang with those that are dumb. Don't waste time because no one is forever young. Grow gracefully. Don't just wither away. You must value and take care of each day. Whatever you want to happen, has to happen in your mind. If I think I will loose the race, I am already behind. Negative and positive thoughts come to life. If you are not listening to me, you may have had your mind made up before I even started to write.

Trust your mind. It is the most popular and most used computer that was ever invented. The mind is always at work even when you are not aware. There is never a power shortage. All you have to do is keep the viruses away. God did a great thing when God created the brain. Even animals have enough brains to use them for survival. Don't under estimate your mind. God did not give it to you just to take up space in your head. Everything that is created is created for a reason. Everything has purpose behind it. The saying of, "something told me that was going to happen" is a true saying because your brain tried to warn you. One of the easiest ways to prove how the mind can work with or without you is the fact that, the mind has dreams. You wake up to talk about it if you can remember it like it was a movie. Your mind does not know what is real or fake. That is why night mares wake some up so easily. Since the mind does not know, it is up to you to program the reality that you want before the reality comes.

I was once asked to be a member of a committee that was put together to try to better my old middle school, "Forest Oak". In this meeting, we came up with different quotes that we were familiar with. A few of the quotes graced the hall ways of the school which is what everyone needs, not just schools. You also need positive reminders at home, at work, in the car, or where ever you are, often. These are a few of the quotes. Act as if what you do makes a difference. It does. When you reach the end of your rope, tie a knot in it and hold on. An ounce of action is worth a ton of theory. You must be the change that you wish to see in the world. If you can not be a poet, be the poem. If you keep your face to the sun shine, you will not see the shadows. The future belongs to those who believe in the beauty of their dreams. Only those who can see the invisible can accomplish the impossible.

Thought is action in rehearsal. The only way around is through. The impossible is often the untried. One who makes no mistakes never makes anything. The journey of a thousand miles begins with one step. Success is a state of mind. Even the longest journey begins with one step. Every great achievement was once considered impossible. Great minds have purpose. Others have wishes. Never give up, never, never, never. (Winston Churchill) Someone's opinion of you does not have to become your reality. Life is short. Make your mark! Look to the future because that is where you are going to spend the rest of your life. Don't count the days. Make the days' count. Every moment is a new beginning. Education is preparation for life. Nothing last forever, not even troubles. Accept no one's definition of your life; define yourself.

Chapter 11

It's Bigger Than Us

Whatever you've learned, it's deeper than that. We are not talking opinions. We are talking facts. It is deeper than whatever we think. It's deeper than bath tubs and sinks. It is deeper than water and oil wells. It is deeper than subliminal messages in fairy tales. It is deeper than the ocean floor. It is deeper than that for sure. To every problem, there is a cure. Your spirit is either evil or pure. What are you doing with your life? Aggravation is hell. Heaven is nice. Something or somebody has to be served. Is it God, money, him or her? We are one; with everything that exist. I know that everyone is not ready for this but this is what I am supposed to write. I think I've been here before; but this time, I am trying to get it right. You have to stop running around here being so "ticked off" about what you don't have. Stop remaining so sad. Stop being so "pissed off". Stop aggravating people on purpose like you are "the law". The image of the Creator is in each of us. Put peace in your life and eliminate the fuss and that is by any means necessary. That may even mean that you have to get away from "John Doe and his wife, Mary".

If the Creator speaks things into existence; you do too since you are in the Creator's image. You have to stay balanced to go the distance. You have to eventually get tired of coming back again. Remember, you are a spirit transported in the form of woman and man but the spirit is in the image of the Creator. What level did you get off on from life's elevator? I know sometimes it feels like you only walk up the stairs and it seems like no one around you really cares. You have to always be prepared. Stop getting off track. If you don't get up, it is not God's fault that you are still on your back. Take care of your business and make sure you watch what you say around those kids. They are always listening and that's just what that is. Children are closer to the Creator than most adults. They are most recently from God. We are the ones that have been exposed to so much other stuff. We have been taught so many different things. Walk by faith and try to forget some of the things that you have seen. Everything makes a 360 cycle. You have to be disciplined to be a disciple. There are many versions you can study of a bible and something is wrong if no one gets revived at your revival. Think before you speak because you can't take back what you have said. It is deeper than whatever you got going on in your head. I mean, you deep but have you ever thought about the universe and how all light has to come from dark first? Disrespecting me is disrespecting yourself and where are your "leech" friends when you need some help? Always try to keep pure thoughts. Control your temper instead of always "going off". You have to put the right pictures in your catalog. You have to try to forget some of the things that you saw.

The news tells us what they want us to know. We are spectators believing whatever they show. We just assume that their report is correct. Do you watch your hours when they give you your check? All of those media alphabets are tied together. Isn't it amazing how some try control the weather? They also control terrorist attacks and some of these natural disasters. Some children are forced into becoming bastards. Some are still following the wrong master. We own no business but we spend money faster. The only reason why we don't have our own is because we were taught to give everyone else some. We have been trained to learn everyone else's language. We think our own culture is dangerous. Some get upset for me talking like this. They say, "don't be too loud. Just hold up your fist. Just use two fingers and make a peace sign. Just keep reading books but don't speak your mind". I am glad that I listen to the "Nameless One" and not you. You and I both have things to do. I'm not gone tell you to quit your job or your dream. I am supposed to follow my dreams if you know what I mean. If I am not, I am not serving my purpose. Your learning should not be worthless. Maybe it is not deep to you and that is perfectly fine but it is still deeper than yours and mine.

I ask about things that no one else ever questions; like, why is malt liquor sold on one side of town and not the other? Why are certain commercials targeted toward certain groups? Why are people in certain groups categorized by their address? Why do you think your culture is better than mine? Why do people fall into certain brackets? Why are people that look like me the biggest consumers but we own so little? Why are the businesses in the "hood" closed down? Why are all super heroes in America Caucasian? The closest America will give you to a Black super hero is, someone like "Hancock". This super hero sleeps under benches, flies drunk with his 40 ounce bottle, tears up the city and resembles a homeless man that dresses warm even when it is hot outside. Why does America glorify people of color when they have done something wrong? Others do things wrong too; however, their situation seems to not receive as much publicity. Why did "New Orleans" really get flooded? Why don't brothers pull their pants up so they can stop walking like "penguins? Is it because they want to be whatever the television tells them to be. The television always tells a vision. Do they know the history behind sagging pants? Do they know that some slaves were not allowed to wear a belt to make it hard to run away and in prison, it represented that you were available to "get stuck" and I am not talking about with a knife? Why is your religion better than mine? Why do the so called, filled with the holy ghost, sanctified, church folks, talk about you in a negative way? I heard a pastor tell his congregation, "We all have broken the rules. We all just didn't get caught, so what makes you better"? Why can't all church folks forgive like they say "Jesus" did? Why isn't the bible still being written? Why do people use phrases like, "You talk white or you acting black"? Why do we still kill ourselves with certain soul food? Most of this food was just left over food or food that the slave master wouldn't eat. Most of your soul food of today is the slave food of yesterday. Why does organic food cost more? What is the real agenda in the education system's school curriculum and why are we so against our "Black" businesses? Why do children in "Texas" have to pass a test to graduate from high school? Why don't we read? Why don't we speak up for what is right? Why do we "mean mug" each other and why don't sorry people ever try harder? You have to try as hard as you can. That is what gets God to notice and appreciate you more. Wouldn't you get tired of forgiving the same person over and over again if they kept doing the same thing over and over again. That is how a lot of us treat God. You have to get in tune with God. The only way you can truly succeed is to understand that you are a piece of a much bigger puzzle but without you, the puzzle will never be complete.

Accept the energy from the universe. This is where it comes from first. For true energy in life, you don't really thirst. Stop believing them when they tell you that you have been cursed. You can make things better but you would rather keep them worse. To receive true energy, does not have to hurt. I am receiving energy from the universe to write this verse. God has blessed us with everything we need but we do not want to grow. We want to remain as seeds. Stop wasting energy on making your brother and sister bleed; furthermore, people bleed more than physically. We argue and fuss which messes each of our minds up, mentally. You get more than what they say you get when you do good deeds. Things that are positive, you should start or continue to read. Sad stories do not do a bit of good so keep them, please. Know that God will listen to you even if you are not on your knees. Always pray and appreciate the grass and the trees. The free energy is right there among the leaves. Always thank the "Nameless One" for the breeze. The breeze reminds us to be thankful for the breaths we breathe. You don't have to eat; but this information, I must feed. People lie to their children like their children can't see. If you don't teach them, they will get taught something from the streets. It is your requirement as an adult to teach. There is no such thing as growing up too fast but you can grow up too wrong and then crash. You have to actually take the test in order to pass. Stop wasting energy, trying to harass. As far as coincidences, those are supposed to happen. When people say things like; "speaking of the devil; we were just talking about you", you just start laughing. You don't correct them. "What did you all say about me", is what you start asking. Call me an angel instead of a devil. If you let God, God will take you to different levels. It is up to you to dig deep like a shovel. Keep your foot on the gas. Mash the petal. Be cautious because if you can watch television, television could be watching you and I know the higher authorities don't want us to know the truth. I have to serve my purpose. I have things to do and remember to always lift up our youth. My mind is just as powerful as yours and yours is just as powerful as mine but the system has trained us to remain behind. They don't want me to tell you this. They want us to stay blind. We have been taught to go crazy over material things and people that are physically fine. Can you imagine what we could do if we would unite and bind. Can you imagine really working your mind? If you can imagine it, that means you can do it. Let positive thoughts flow through you like fluid.

Do you think that the "Creator" was just creating things for art work? If any of the pieces are missing, the picture is not complete. Animals are part of the picture. We are part of the picture too. The tree has to be here as well as the flowers and plants. They are needed for our survival. You must have the different seasons. God is in everything and every moment. The "Creator" is so awesome. Think about how important a bee is. Without the bee, man gets no honey. The plants and flowers don't get pollinated. Not only that but the sun rises every day and the Earth turns. They say there are as many stars as there are grains of sand on a beach. There are other planets and galaxies. God is way bigger than we can even imagine but I enjoy trying to learn about the Creator's creation. These are a few examples and hopefully, you can understand. It is up to you. "God" does not move for you until you move for yourself.

We are not waiting on "God". "God" is waiting on us. We procrastinate everyday but we always want "God" to rush. "Lord, help me pay my car note and my rent. Let me find some money on the ground because all of my money is spent. Lord, please don't let them fire me today." Would your church be upset if you helped someone that needed it with some of those tithes that you pay? When is the last time you helped someone? You walk to see "God" but to the drama, you run. You are just waiting on "God" to send you a blessing. Be careful because "God" does not need testing. "God" sees and knows everything you do. Just because your pastor does not know what you do, does not mean that "God" does not see you. When you don't give from the heart, don't think that "God" doesn't know. It is totally up to you, to grow. Your back is against the wall so now you are praying like you never prayed before. At the same time, you are steady letting the wrong people come through your door. "I know "God" is going to bless me with some good presents for Christmas." Many treat "God" like a "genie". They are steady making wishes. "Dear Lord, let me hit the lottery. Dear Lord, I will not drink any more. Make it stop. I shouldn't have come to this party". We are not waiting on "God". "God" is waiting on us. We procrastinate everyday but we always want "God" to rush.

You are in "God's" image, so "God" does not appreciate you being so sorry. You must put forth some type of effort. We have been taught that stuff will just fall out of the sky. This is not true. You have to put in the work and ask "God" to help you. Do not waste "God's" time by wasting your own time. Believe me; "God" is going to be alright with or without you. Do yourself a favor and let the "God" in you be the "God" in you.

This is what I had to tell "God". "Alright "God", I'm back. I am getting ready to act like I am supposed to act. Like the side walk, I have cracked. I know I need to pick up the slack. I'm frustrated but I bet a whole lot of people can say that. I know "God" is working on me for a fact. Instead of pleasing "God", I've been trying to impress "Jane and Jack". "In the game", my money never did really "stack". Everything that goes on with me, I attract. I need your insurance "God", not "Gico or Aflack". You can't stay a "hamburger". You have to eventually become a "big mac"! Super size your order with "God", free of tax. I am going to stop waiting till it's rough to talk to "God". I will talk to "The Most High" even when I relax. I know I must give the "Creator" praise and credit to the max. I have not been exercising my faith like jumping jacks. I have to take my thinking cap off of the rack. I always want to talk to "God" when I am doing bad but I know I am supposed to talk even when I am glad. There is no reason to tell you that I am sad. I only have myself to blame. I can't blame you "Mom and Dad". There is no reason to be so mad. I am the reason why I don't have cash. I am the reason why I lost what I had. I am the reason why I don't act right and choose to act bad. I am the one that has been skipping, and not going to class. I'm the one that has been living life way too fast. It is my own fault that I have crashed. I stay too quiet about you. I need to keep you "on blast". I am through waiting till I am sick like the television show, "Mash". I know this is a marathon but I act like it is a hundred-yard dash. I know to win the race; I can't continue to lag. I act like I want to crash. I try to store you and use you when I need you like a "drive flash". I act like you will not bless me with everything I ask. Sometimes, I act like "God" is dead like "dust to dust and ash to ash". Let me end it with this "hash tag". I'm back "God", so can I once again, get a pass?

We often forget how we got as far as we have gotten. We forget that we used to talk to "God" every day when we did not have a job or we had no food to eat. We used to talk all the time when we had nowhere to stay or when we got scared. At twenty-one years of age, "God" helped me learn one of my most valuable lessons. I was broke, had no place to stay, and was hungry. I talked to "God" every-day especially when I was walking and waiting on buses. You have so much time to yourself in these moments. I prayed and meditated. Then I meditated and prayed some more. I was thanking "God" for everything in my life. I thanked "God" for waking me up, letting the grass be green, the sky being blue, for family, and feet to walk to work when I got my job. I was just as thankful for the little things as I was for the big things. God blessed me. In a years' time, I bought a car, got a house on a few acres of land, and started working for a major com-pany and making a nice size check every week. Then I started acting like I made all of that happen on my own. I started treating "God" like "God" and been locked up in jail. I was not putting anything on "God's books". I was not praying. I started saying, "I did this and I did that." The next thing you know, I totaled my car, burnt up a borrowed car, went to jail, lost my job, and got evicted. All this happened in one month. What I had been blessed with in a years' time, I lost in one month. Then I got back to the basics as we all tend to do; but this time, I will stick to the basics. I loved talking to "God" again. We have a one on one relationship, just like you. I will never forget my true pro-vider and friend again.

"Lord", give me guidance. I am not really sure of which way to go. Way to often, I have said "yes" when it should have been "no". I know that I started taking credit for your actions. I apologize and guid-ance is what I am now asking. I know you heard me before I even had this thought. I was trying to be "slick; ya dig, and got caught. I know you are the reason for the season and it was you that I was teasing. You have already blessed me with so many things of material. I stopped saying thank you and they disappeared like cereal, going into a young child's mouth. I have gone north when I should have gone south. I went left when I should have gone right. I have stayed in the darkness. "Dear Lord", show me the light. Help me recognize my foe and my friend. Once again; "Lord", please just help me begin and I promise to work a lot harder than last time. Help guide me in these words of rhyme. Bless me with the ability to not talk behind mans' back. Help me keep my voice down and learn to live with the facts. Help me to keep a smile on my face. With time, remind me not to waste because I can't be here and do the things I do without you. Help me recognize the difference between false and true and bless me to choose true every time it comes about. Help me keep my voice down and no longer shout. I am nothing unless I am on your team. Guide me through reality and through my dreams. I know I am running my mouth a whole lot. I just want to make sure that when it is all said and done, I am in the right spot. Help me keep this happiness, peace, and love. I know you have work for me if they say you had work for a dove. When I speak to others, help me to make sure I keep you in the con-versation. "Lord", I am just asking you to help guide me through my situations. "Lord", give me guidance.

I am through trying to do it on my own. All the ones that have gone before me to become a success have always told me to put "God" first. I did put "God" first on the outside. I never missed church or any church function. I put my "front on" for the church folks. The whole time, I was trying to impress the wrong people. I was worried about what the church folks thought. I acted like "God" didn't know I was messing up. "I knew the stove would burn my hand if I touched it but I touched it anyway." Every time I do something that I am not supposed to do, I know it. My conscious tells me, "You know you are wrong for this one". See, "God" knows what is going on with me no matter what I say or look like on the outside. It does not matter how hard I shout or testify. It does not matter how well I sound when I lead the choir. "God" knows me when I am by myself. "The Nameless One" wants to guide you if you will allow that to happen. It is totally up to you.

I graduated from religion. I was a "magnum kum lade" Christian. Don't get me wrong because Christianity does make you a better you. All I am saying is, "can you prove that everything you teach me is the truth". It does not make it true because you tell me what you think you know. All my life; all I ever wanted to do was grow. I grew up in a church that always said, "no". They called some visiting ladies a "jazzy bell" after they taught us that "Jazzy" was a hoe (whore). I was taught that the television was a "one eyed devil". Women couldn't wear ear rings or make up and still go to "Heaven". Women could not wear pants or shorts. You also went to "hell" if you smoked, "Kools, Virginia Slims, Basics, Winstons, Camels, Black and Milds, or New Ports". You basically were not allowed to smoke or drink. I was brain washed on how to think. There is a chance that you might not get your "white wings or your white robe". They taught not to judge but for some reason, they already knew that "God" said "no". We could not go to parties or listen to secular radio stations. When you tell a kid "no", you create more temptation. I asked my mom about this and she taught me that it was church doctrine. I do not apologize but I will never be part of the flock again. I got grown and was still searching for the truth because I stopped believing everything that I was taught in my youth. I have been "Pentecostal, Non-Denominational, Methodist, and Baptist; when in reality, I was really just practicing "Roman Catholic". I have had questions that no one could seem to answer. Men were not allowed to have long hair but they taught me about "Jesus and Samson". Once again; as most stories in the bible, a woman made "Samson" fall; just like when "Eve gave Adam" the "red ball" from the life knowledge tree, that makes my daughter a sinner before she even is born to me. They say everybody has to pay for what "Eve" did. "Eve" messed up so, that makes my baby be born into sin. That is a bunch of "bull corn". The children are most recently from "God". They were just born. Plus, "Eve of the bible" was not by herself. Adam was there to do his part in this so called sinners step. I've been told that "Jesus" is coming back real soon but it surely seems as if it is taking a long time. I am not trying to be funny but someone has to be lying. I graduated from the thing that keeps us separate and makes us hate each other. I graduated from religion. Now I am in graduate school, really working on my God given spirit.

I know all churches are not anything like the one that I was brought up in as a child. I do know that I was in one of the strictest churches ever in the history of churches but I think they are all alike in other obvious ways. Some people go to church to be a part of the fashion show. As a kid, I was almost ready to go to "hell" because it was too hard to go to "Heaven". I've had questions for pastors and I was always given "made up" answers because they did not know the answer. Trying not to be embarrassed, they would tell me anything because they are supposed to have an answer for everything. If they had told me that they didn't know, that would have a least been the truth. I do not need to go through any man to talk to "God". What is the purpose for having different religions anyway if we are all talking about the same "God"? Why can't the Baptist church fellowship with the Catholic for example? Truth be told, church is the one place left that is still segregated. Why do they have the apocrypha in some bibles and not in others and why doesn't anyone learn the history of your beloved "King James"? In the words of "2 Pac", only "God" can judge me.

I am that I am. Don't I have the right to say that as a man? You can't tell me that I am in God's image, then act like this is just a scrimmage. I am the real deal and this one counts. God is in me by the pound, not just an ounce. I am God. Am I not? I know you want to send me to a place that is hot. That place only exists in your head because someone taught you what your bible said. Prove it since you know all of the false facts. You can't even prove where Heaven is at or what it looks like. You think that everything you say is right and I am wrong if I do not agree. You burn yours up but you want me to love my enemy. You try to speak for God like I don't talk to God. I stay tuned in like an i-pod. I know you think I am blasphemy on this one. Jesus of the bible is not God's only son. I am one of God's sons too. Can you prove that everything you think is true? No, you can't but I know you will not stop. You have your mind made up, don't you? I accept that but you do not have the only truth. You can't prove it no matter how many scriptures you recite. Maybe, we are both right. I know you don't think so. With that type of thinking, you can no longer grow. You can't possibly know it all. It is bigger than us. Don't make God short. God is tall. God is forever so why do you try to bring the world to an end. We are supposed to help complete what God begins.

We are spiritual beings having human experiences. Do you really think you are just flesh and bones? You keep walking around here like "Earth" is your final home. It's whatever with you because you are having fun. You don't belong to you. We are "God's" daughters and sons. We wait to call on "God" when we get in trouble. We are supposed to love our sisters and brothers. You were not scientifically or mechanically made. You are supposed to be in graduate school but you can't get out the first grade. Where is your faith? Eliminate negative spirits from your space. Use your entire mind. Making you, "God" didn't waste his and her time. You have the ability to make mountains move. What spirit will you choose? You have to choose one. You must live until your purpose is done.

Think past the mind of man. We are in "God's" image so what don't you understand? "God's plan is bigger than your plan for you. Man will lie but "God" always tells the truth. You have to do what you can before "God" will do what you cain't. You are worth more than the account at your bank. Talk to "God" before you get in a mess. Talk to "God" before the stress. Talk to "God" before the problem. Read more bible verses and less news columns. Stay away from negative people. In the wrong environment, you don't want to linger, because you become your environment. You have to work toward your retirement and I am not talking about the job. I am talking about your retirement with "God". We are spiritual beings having human experiences. Can the church say "a-men or ase"? Can I get a witness? You can accomplish more than you think. Without "God", your eyes can not even blink. You can't even breathe, ya dig. You can't even grow or get big. You can't do anything without the "Supreme Being". You have to see past what your physical eyes are seeing. You have to get your mind right. You have to look into your inner sight. You have to converse with the "Creator" at all times. You have to strive to become divine. You have to eventually get it right. Follow "God" like they teach you to follow "Christ". We are all a part of "God's living word". To get to the seventh level, you have to get past the third. You are a spiritual being. Always see past what your physical eyes are seeing.

You are a spirit inside of some human flesh. It is bigger than you and I. We are all a part of "God's" great work and all "God" wants us to do is cooperate with the program that "God" has provided. Stop believing everything a man tells you. You better talk to "God" as often as you can. Man can be hard to find but "God" never is. "God" is always right there with you. Don't be disrespectful toward "God". Show "God" your appreciation. "God" appreciates this and "God" is the only one who can really understand what you are going through. "God" wants you to trust him and her so you can move to the next level in the beautiful plan.

Paul "Phroze" Munson

Biography

Paul Munson; also known as, "Phroze" was born in 1976. He has always been a class act in more ways than one. Paul witnessed poetry being recited at an early age by his mother. He wrote his first works of poetry when he was in the 5th grade. (He still has those writings today) Munson graduated from "O.D. Wyatt High School" and attended "Texas Southern University". Writing was and still is his main outlet. He said, when no one else wants to hear him, the paper always listens. "Phroze" started back writing in 1996. Shortly after that, he was introduced to open mics. "Phroze" attended as many as possible. He has been a guest speaker at various venues around the metroplex. By the year 2000, he was hosting talent shows. Paul has recorded 3 albums from 2000 until 2007. "Phroze" also created personalized greeting cards and framed poetry. This is his first of many books. Read and enjoy.

Acknowledgements

First and foremost, I would like to acknowledge "God"; the Creator of the universe, for creating me. I would like to acknowledge my Queen, Angela for being my best friend. I salute both of my daughters, "Ale'gna' and Serenity" for believing that I can do anything. Much love goes to my parents, "Levi and Susan" for being two of the best role models in the world. I celebrate my brothers and sister, "RaTem, Les, and Shirl for always having my back throughout the years. I would like to acknowledge A.J. Houston, Devie Perry, and Michael Jordan for their help with this project. A special shout out goes to "Future Star Studios" and the engineer, "Gent" for helping me create the audio for this book. Last but not least, I would like to acknowledge you for your support. Thank you so much.

Contact Information:

Facebook: Paul Phroze Munson

Instagram: phrozethegreat

For Booking:

mrpauldmunson@att.net

Thank you for your support